FIELDER'S CHOICE

Fielder's Choice

Elise Partridge

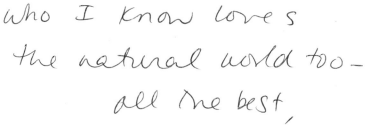

For Sue
who I know loves
the natural world too —
all the best,
Elise Partridge

Signal
EDITIONS

SIGNAL EDITIONS IS AN IMPRINT OF VÉHICULE PRESS

Published with the generous assistance of The Canada Council for the
Arts and the Book Publishing Industry Development Program of the
Department of Canadian Heritage.

Signal Editions editor: Carmine Starnino
Cover design: David Drummond
Photograph of the author: Marjorie Tompkins
Typeset in Minion by Simon Garamond
Printed by AGMV-Marquis Inc.

CANADIAN CATALOGUING IN PUBLICATION DATA

Partridge, Elise
Fielder's choice / Elise Partridge.

Poems.
ISBN 1-55065-170-6

I. Title.
PS8581.A7665F44 2002   C811'.6   C2002-904976-8
PR9199.4.P373F44 2002

Published by Véhicule Press, Montréal, Québec, Canada
www.vehiculepress.com

Distribution in Canada by LPG Distribution
Distributed in the U.S. by Independent Publishers Group

Printed and bound in Canada.

For Steve

verray parfit

Acknowledgements

I would like to thank the editors of the following journals in which these poems have appeared, often in different forms and with different titles: *AGNI, Alaska Quarterly Review, Books in Canada, Boulevard, Cimarron Review, The Cream City Review, DoubleTake, The Fiddlehead, The Malahat Review, The New Republic, Notre Dame Review, Poetry Ireland Review, Poetry Northwest, www.Slate.com, The Southern Review, Tar River Poetry, The Tennessee Review, TickleAce.*

"Rural Route" and "Pauper, Boston, 1988" first appeared in *Poetry.*

"Two Monuments" was published on the Yeats Society of New York website (2001 Competition).

Deep debts are attested to in several poems' dedications. I want to thank my mother, Marjorie Townsend Tompkins, for patience, encouragement, and always being willing to read; my family and friends for many kindnesses, especially while I completed this manuscript over the past year; the Vancouver Poetry Dogs, for raucous discussions; and the nurses, doctors and staff at the British Columbia Cancer Agency. Thanks also to the British Columbia Festival of the Arts (Penticton, 1996). And to my editor, Carmine Starnino: thank you for being enthusiastic, blunt, and undaunted.

Contents

ONE

Everglades 11
Plague 12
Phoenixville Farm 14
Arcadia 16
Two Sketches from a Peaceable Kingdom 17
The Artists' House 19
August 21
Spring 22
In the Barn 23
Caught 24
A Valediction 25
One Calvinist's God 26
Gnomic Verses from the Anglo-Saxon 27

TWO

The Secret House 31
For a Father 33
Pauper, Boston, 1988 34
To a Flicker Nesting in a Telephone Pole 36
On the Road to Emmaus 37
Rural Route 39
1959 40
Elegy 41
Group Portrait 42
Three Women, Nursing Home, Medical Wing 44
Two Monuments 46
Ways of Going 47
The Book of Steve 48
Epitaph for Diane 54
Dislocations 55

THREE

Insights 59
Rejection-Slip Rumba 61
Inspiration 62
Publish or Perish 64
Unknown Artists 65
Temp 67
Supermarket Scanner 69
Exile 71
Four Lectures by Robert Lowell, 1977 73
Philosophical Arguments 76
Display Case, County Museum, Washington State 78
Two Scenes from Philadelphia 79
Ruin 80
Odysseys 82

NOTES 85

ONE

EVERGLADES

Nothing fled when we walked up to it,
nor did we flinch,
even at the hobnailed gators sunning two-inch fangs,
a licorice-whip snake slipping over our shoes.
The normally secretive clapper-rail
appeared under our boardwalk
glancing this way and that,
casual as a moviegoer hunting for a seat.
Tropical, temperate, each constituency spoke —
the sunburned-looking gumbo-limbo trees
nodded side by side with sedate, northern pines.
Even the darkness gave its blessing
for the moonflower to open under its aegis.
A bird swaying on a pole of sedge
sang two notes that might have been "Name me."

PLAGUE

.Heal-all, angelica, alum-root,
yarrow, sweet Annie, valerian shoots —
swinging under foxgloves' lavender bells
a secret to make a sick heart well —
at that eastern farm we waded flowers
and herbs renowned for their healing powers.
Black-eyed Susans in orange beds,
yellow primroses nodded their heads
as I followed the signs into the wood.
It was plicking, dim, laundry-room humid;
mosquitoes like dust-motes blown into flight
almost haphazardly settled to bite.
Two pinks caught my eye. Bending down,
I saw a caterpillar going to town
on a faltering stem; its body was slung
underneath, like a sloth's; the feet clung;
the head chewed. Four were making a meal
beneath a spray of Solomon's-seal
whose white drops kept quivering. Paired prongs,
their six front legs worked like icemen's tongs,
curving to stab. The rear-guard pylons,
gray, flat-soled, ten dutiful cousins,
helped shiver along the elegant back,
red and blue pustules edged with black.
Veering into a sunny aisle
— magenta bee-balm, white chamomile —
I saw dozens more, tan heads like helmets
bobbing over the lambs-ears' velvet.
These maidenhair ferns were brewed for tea
to soothe a sore throat, cure pleurisy —
their two-inch, humping, whiskered lines
were even strewn on the naturalists' signs.
They sprawled under the spindly buds

of red-root, used to strengthen the blood;
a jewelweed's freckled orange scoops
hung over gnawed leaves; a spicebush drooped;
this wake-robin looked pocked, that ginger torn,
violets' poulticing sprouts had been shorn,
betonys' too — I could find no leaf
that hadn't already come to grief.
Running down the path, now I could see
they were pasted to the bole of every tree;
the plicking I'd thought was rain in my ears
sounded like snips of miniature shears —
their migrant, hungry, adhering strips
made, as I stood there, sawtoothed rips
in thousands more seedlings. Soon
they'd each find a twig and start to spin;
one moon-rise not too far from this,
fresh from a cracking chrysalis,
their tawny, fluttering selves would come
tilting to this wild geranium,
alight on finer, fewer legs
and discharge arsenals of eggs.

PHOENIXVILLE FARM

Each subdivision lawn bore the same shrubs
with minor variations — scraggly, full —
and timid bands of housefinches we glimpsed
through curtains drawn to protect chintz parterres.
Each spring every family on the block
would weed-whack, edge, clip, prune, spray, rototill,
fumigate ants, squash snails. And each fall,
rakes would be jabbed and dragged through balding yards,
leaves crammed in plastic bags for Sanitation.
Indoors, forced narcissi sat on sills
by velvet-napped violets; off-white walls wore
oils of red-coated hunters clutching whips.
Guppies flicked bored beside their plastic castles;
bored to anxiety, gerbils quaked in tanks.
We ate peas dribbled from cans, pale canned pear-halves,
sogged blobs of peaches in viscous syrup.
The change of seasons was marked by switching off
or on the central AC's monotone thrum.

But at Anne's, nothing was mowed; Queen-Anne's lace
bobbed all over her yard. Buck, her tick-prone hound,
set our agenda, baying us around the farm.
We'd sprawl in wild mustard, withers to withers,
companionable as old cows; breathe deep
skunkcabbage-reek from chartreuse scum-slick ponds
where frogs with hurdlers' thighs zapped flies and belched.
Hawks tensed above us. We gobbled blackberries
off stabbing vines, smearing our faces purple,
sucked dandelion milk. We warmed wet hands
in the hunter's belly-fur, gouged clean the hoof
that had shattered a rib; watched lambs yank udders;
tried to nurse fledglings, their bodies tufted lumps
of wrinkled dough, each eye a bugging bruise.

A hen might shriek up from a garbage can;
we'd stroke four fresh eggs in a slide of feed.
Burnt-orange flashing in the back field —
a fox, glaring: What are you doing here?
Anne showed us how to scoop a bludgeoning hornet
with one palm from a pane and fling it free,
how baby spiders rappelled down a shed wall.
At dusk the bats that were dangling like berets
from the barn eaves chittered through sycamores;
one moon-white night we chirred around the yard
after a trundling family of raccoons,
the pond throbbing with peepers, *here here here here.*
When parents came next morning to pick us up,
we lay like glossy eggplants in the garden,
white sneakers gobbed with dung. We wanted to hide
like spitbugs in fizzing clots, tuck ourselves in
all winter under a pinecone's sticky eaves.
Some day, some day — we'd each spin sleeping bags,
doze for six weeks, thrust, gnaw, unkink striped wings,
try out our newborn feelers, lurch to Anne's farm,
bathe in dust puddles, lay eggs, and worship weeds.

ARCADIA

Everything at your farm was new to me —
nub-wing ducklings tipping around a nest;
leaf-hands extended from a sassafras tree;

and even guineahens seemed charming there —
shrieking across the yard, dewlaps flapping,
while the shepherd mutt dozed in his chair.

I learned, that summer, not just to walk by
when hummingbirds backpedaled in air
catching the sweetness from a flower's eye;

to notice what I'd never have seen
without your love — fields seared for second growth;
a beetle gleaming like Thai silk, turquoise-green.

TWO SKETCHES FROM A PEACEABLE KINGDOM

1. *Whale-Watching*

A grinning band —
barnacled dripping chins,
jaws as broad
as a tugboat's bumper;

black backs,
glossy, rolling —
white fins like sails
smack the horizon,

forked tails
flip. . . .
One leaps, klutzy, lunging,
snorting, as if for joy.

2. *Weaving*

Just outside our door,
a hall stacked with skeins:
spiders bridge one corner —
hexagon stripes

tug lightly at guy-wires,
banners billow at their ease.
Inside the studio,
red weft,

blue warp,
we clack wooden shuttles,
pound pedals
on our looms —

two sets of workers
alone and at peace,
separated only
by a swinging door.

THE ARTISTS' HOUSE

for Ruth K. Fackenthal

Their peeling porch was shaded by bamboo,
a talkative, clacking stand.
The scruffy yard was strewn with cinderblocks —
stages for minstrel flocks
of cardinals, robins, jays.
Under her tire swing, daylilies grew.
We navigated the rhododendron's maze
where Ruth could cup a bumblebee in one hand;
we braided lanyards out of plantain shoots,
watched spiders spinning eggsacs between the beech's roots.

Inside, Ruth's whole family hung on the walls.
In the study Uncle Clint,
unfinished, clutched a glove, a blob of white.
The house wore forest-twilight,
its air tangy with paint.
The upstairs ambled off in crooked halls,
the door to one hung with a crack-faced saint,
the other with a Rauschenberg aquatint.
Ivy crept under one sill across the floor
where swathed old couches sat like longboats on a shore.

The kitchen paper revealed, beneath its flaps,
two plaster continents nudging,
a giant with a dozen bulging eyes.
There we boiled black dye,
yellowed a sweatshirt with bark tea,
pinched flour-and-water mixtures into maps:
a lopsided Mount Everest, twin galaxies.
We improvised mobiles — blown eggs and string;
dabbed posterboard with paint-smeared slices of limes;
built masks for Halloween out of paste and shredded *Times*.

On freezer wrap we traced a mushroom's spores;
under the blurry lens
of her junior microscope we squinted at stalks,
eyelashes, slivers of chalk.
Mornings we overheard
her mother humming through her studio door;
sometimes we'd catch a word.
Each day we got out pastels, charcoal, pens
and India inks — Ruth had them in every hue —
boarded the longboats, chose our colors, hummed, and drew.

AUGUST

Late August night,
I'm dozing in bed —

crickets sturdily cheeping —
elm nodding its head —

suddenly, *flare!*
glaring swath —

star, plummeting —
singed path.

If only some giant
had tossed that huge ball

through galaxy air —
if it hadn't fallen

and snuffed itself out
blazing along its arc,

but lay safe, nestled
in a glove in the dark

(a fireproof mitt:
thick clouds, congealed) —

the fielder pivoting
at the edge of the field. . . .

SPRING

Up from evergreens' writhing roots

    as if by a needle deftly drawn

the natty snake winds in between

        sprigs and buds on the forest floor;

over Solomon's-seal and lily shoots

    through dangling bleeding-hearts pulled on,

flattening staffs of fiddlehead fern,

        dividing every pledge to green.

IN THE BARN

One morning, on the mud floor of the barn,
we found a snake glittering in the sun —
ten inches patterned like an argyle sock,
black diamonds on gray. Puffing beside his neck

was a red bubble. No — wait — then we saw
he had a frog clamped in his propped jaw.
The bubble was blood. The frog sat elbows-out,
impassive, an old magistrate in court

hearing a plea. His skin was mottled brown,
dark mud splattered on light. His eyes were open,
gold-rimmed, fixed. He blinked; the eyes looked moist.
His neck bulged; the oversized mouth seemed set.

Desperate-eyed, the cows stared up at us,
clinking linked chains, swaying in their stalls.
The snake glanced sideways, but he couldn't budge,
avid, like we were, edging nearer to watch.

At last the frog looked uncomfortable,
as though trying to be dignified. Wilful,
the snake was helpless too, frog jamming his jaw.
We ran when a calf started to bawl.

CAUGHT

One wing-tip was stuck to one silk thread.
He ran his six legs through thin air
like a cartoon character,
wrenching
his abdomen to his jerking head.

But the shivering web wouldn't give way.
It had been spun in a couple of hours,
wired casually to a flower.
The fly
writhed above the vetch for half a day.

The spinner was nowhere to be found.
A woodchuck had ripped the web at dawn,
the spider long since skittered on.
He'd start
a new web, elsewhere, once the sun went down.

The glued fly kept flailing. He rubbed his eyes,
kicked himself into a tiny ball,
a trapeze artist, swung loose, fell —
snagged, on
the lowest strand. Twirled; hung, as if surprised.

A VALEDICTION

Thump on the roof.
The owl again?
Rising short shrieks —
mouse? rat?
I counted ten.

Terrified yelps
squeezed by a talon.
To have that be
your final say!
And your last vision

looming feathers,
diving beak.
Clutched, wriggling,
squeaking —
speak!

What was he crying —
"Mother, help me"?
"Have mercy on me,
Eli, Eli"?
"I am not ready"?

Neck snapped, dangling;
a moment: taken.
Hamlet wouldn't
kill Claudius, so.
Too small a ration.

Foraging, scrabbling,
snatched; plea.
Hunching wings,
wad of bones
spat under a tree.

Your deity was as patient as a heron,
watching and waiting, as if he could stand for a week
without trembling once on those old-man's legs;
then with one jab of his beak

stab you and gulp. Or, a bald eagle, he'd hunch
on a pine snag or barnacled dais of rock,
scowling, scanning the shore for a newborn duck
to scoop from the flock.

Even the hopping robin who tilted one eye
as though listening at blades of grass put you on guard,
in case he should snap you, wormlike, a writhing thread
from your white-fenced yard.

One midnight, you imagine, you'll be swept up,
a mouse off a toadstool, shrieking into the air;
gathered by icepick talons to his tweedy chest,
his yellow-eyed glare.

GNOMIC VERSES FROM THE ANGLO-SAXON

[adapted and selected]

Kings shall rule kingdoms. Winter cold is keenest,
summer sun the most searing,
fall freest with her hand. Fate is almighty,
the old are wisest. Jewels must stand upright
in winking bezels, blades break on helmets,
hawks hunch on the glove, the huffing boar
wander the woods with the wretched wolf.
Salmon spawn in northernmost streams,
the king in his castle gives his cronies rings,
bears haunt the heath, the hastening water
floods the rolling fields of the downs.
Lovers meet in secret, monsters skulk
in the swamp, stars seed the sky.
The troop stands together, a glorious band.
Light lunges at dark, life parries death,
good clashes with evil, the old with the young,
army against army battles for the land;
all of us wait in the Lord's arms
for the decree he ordains, darkly, in secret.
Only God knows where our souls will go.

TWO

THE SECRET HOUSE

Then is it sin
To rush into the secret house of death
Ere death dare come to us?
        –Shakespeare, *Antony and Cleopatra*, IV.xv.80-2.

Could yours be the Greek Revival façade
glimpsed through this moss-draped avenue of oaks?
The upper-porch balusters are knocked out like teeth,
starlings circle chipped ceiling medallions.
I thought I heard footsteps —
it must have been a deer
startling itself on the old springhouse floor.
By dawn the whole estate was repossessed by fog.

Or maybe it's the farmhouse off the interstate
with a roof like a squashed hat,
a stoop defended by blackberry bramble.
Straw juts from the second-floor eaves,
stained floursack curtains sag in one window.
In the back field I found a tractor, its seat a rusty scoop,
marooned by a barn unshingling itself.

Perhaps you've moved to some spectral subdivision —
buff garage doors, anonymous shrubs,
airconditioners exhaling,
TVs exuding polar-cap blues.
I heard one car snuffle off, thought I saw blinds jiggling.
Your house might be any one in the series,
impassive behind its interchangeable mailbox.

I hope that it's the place you've always longed for —
clapboard, ramshackle, gabled,
views of a sapphire chip of bay,

goldfinches tussling in the lilac bush.
A swing sways on your white front porch,
your threadbare sneaks awry below it,
an aria spirals out a side window,
friends are laughing in your exuberant garden.

I hold my breath approaching the door,
wondering if you'll welcome me.
But it's too dark for me to see inside,
and only blackbirds answer my call.

FOR A FATHER

Remember after work you grabbed our skateboard,
crouched like a surfer, wingtips over the edge;
wheels clacketing down the pocked macadam,
you veered almost straight into the neighbor's hedge?
We ran after you laughing, shouting, Wait!

Or that August night you swept us to the fair?
The tallest person boarding the ferris wheel,
you rocked our car right when we hit the apex
above the winking midway, to make us squeal.
Next we raced you to the games, shouting, Wait!

At your funeral, relatives and neighbors,
shaking our hands, said, "So young to have died!"
But we've dreamt you're just skating streets away,
striding the fairgrounds toward a wilder ride.
And we're still straggling behind, shouting, *Wait* — !

PAUPER, BOSTON, 1988

The landlady got no reply
that April day when she stopped by,
rapping on the grimy steel door
— Washington Way, Apartment 4,

"senior housing" — gray concrete,
sixteen storeys, honking street,
scabbed dumpster hulking just outside.
Security came. The tenant had died

approximately three days before,
according to the coroner.
Housing notified his VA,
and the funeral home, Francis Shea,

who did city cases for set fees.
Management changed the lock and keys;
Maintenance was dispatched to clear
the rooms where he had lived five years.

(No one knew the man's history —
he'd said he had no family
that could be traced; that he used to box;
worked in a factory gluing clocks;

had breakdowns, wound up in the street.
A cop had noticed his swollen feet
month after month, and finally called
someone in Housing at City Hall.)

It took a day to get the place clean.
At the end they'd filled thirteen
trashcan liners; then they tossed his bed,
scattering armfuls of moldy bread

to curious pigeons. The Veterans
sank a flag by his prepaid stone.
The City paid the last of his rent;
Housing recycled his documents.

Your beak's day begins at six.
I see you crisply discarding splinters,
rounding that gouge
into a welcoming door.

But how could you have chosen this ex-tree —
requisitioned, positioned, slashed, gashed, bolted
like Frankenstein's head?
Wouldn't you rather cling where the calliope-chime of stars
won't be blared away by sodium bulbs?
Whistle from a tower that adds to itself, ring after ring,
whose seed-pod odysseys
mime your fledglings' gift of flight?
Here you will oversee no soft green debuts,
no flaming valedictions.
This ramrod cannot welcome guests —
epiphytes so helpful they're asked to stay forever —
nor be caressed by a million grubs' feet.
Turkeytail fungus
will never ladder to your perch like steps to heaven.

Yet on you build.
Can your defiance proliferate —
this pole claim kin to a nearby maple,
wake one morning urging phantom tendrils
to crack the macadam?
Will your raps remind us to uncommodify —
though dragooned and propped, dream of leafing;
pared by use, cradle eggs?

ON THE ROAD TO EMMAUS

[from a sixteenth-century Flemish painting]

1. *The Painting*

Over the disciples' shoulders
Jesus listens,
eyebrows raised to his hairline, bemused and sad.
Behind them, arched gateways, insouciant pennants;
a pale-blue harbor with minuscule ships,
ochre city, jumble of turrets.
A white-aproned woman in a farmhouse door
chats with a caller;
two men stride off on branching roads,
one trailed by a dawdling child.

2. *The Disciples*

It was a long walk.
Only a few gulps of stale water
slosh around their gourd. Their scalps itch.
Cranky, yawning, shuffling along,
they come upon a man robed in white
and start to explain the entire fiasco:
the nails' heft, the burglar groaning,
how gray He looked when they eased Him down.
How, on that third morning,
birds had darted
restlessly; how one disciple had pictured Jesus
hovering over all His flocks,
Pilate's house halved
by a thunderbolt, centurions claiming
they'd only been following somebody's orders.
Bobbing donkeys, squashed pomegranate-rind —
fifty yards from the tomb's mouth:

"The boulder's gone!"
They edged inside, eyes straining
to adjust from glare.
Black walls dribbled, clay oozed
through their toes. Peering,
they saw ants ferrying chunks of fig.
A crumpled sheet; whiff of myrrh.

On the way to Emmaus the arguments started.
Each turned over and
over particulars.
"I think we've been taken."
You know, nodded the other, I was never really sure.

3. *Always on the Road*

Why did the painter locate them here,
even including a hatpin-height steeple?
Unto the nth generation, he seems to say,
we'll be complaining to the miracle's face
that it is no miracle,
we'll insist to life eternal, "There is no such thing!"
But the tree he placed the disciples under
means more than the sum of its plain brown leaves.
The city's gates swing wide for the asking,
the harbor beckons you to a new life.
That woman in the farmhouse door
loves the man she is speaking to;
her soul has opened to meet his.
The child is a blessing to all of them,
the dust on the road cleanses the sparrows.

He picked three dozen quarts, starting at dawn;
died suddenly in the garden. "Around one,
he had a stroke — I found him, but he was gone — ."
He left a widow, three daughters and six sons.

Two days later, widow and children, at dawn,
picked forty dozen. They ate, washed, dressed;
buried him in the churchyard just after one.
Early the next day, they picked the rest.

1959

In the basement:
damp black linoleum, mildewed walls.
But freshly-washed diapers whiten this table.
Clean will reign!
The woman who never raises her voice
launches her whole weight
into scouring a stain.

Her hissing iron
lunges over a scrap of white.
Left, right, left, right,
tight little jabs at the corners
subduing a handkerchief
into a perfect square.
She holds it up like a banner,
aligns it on a stack.
There.
She seizes a crumpled shirttail.

All day,
the spigot weeps, pipes keen;
and, in the dryer's window, arms flail.

ELEGY

Sixty years I've lived, hardly a cross word said!
(The carpenter found, behind their bed,
a crawl-space where black snakes had bred.)

Each of the Ten Commandments, I kept.
(Broom jabbing, she frantically swept
at filth that flowered while she slept.)

No one can ever say I told lies.
(She faded below her cracking disguise,
fixed as a dead-leaf butterfly's.)

I gave my love to each and all.
(Hoarded in a locked closet down the hall
hatreds muffled by a paisley shawl.)

I never let myself complain.
(Gallons of tears, a wet winter's rain,
whirled at the brim of the churning drain.)

I had the life I wanted to have.
(She stepped unborn into her grave.)

GROUP PORTRAIT

for Lucy, Miriam, and Marjorie

Great-grandmothers in stern black shoes,
frowning in photos at the beach,
the granddaughter you raised still lives
within your wagging fingers' reach.

One widowed too young, one who mopped
parquet floors as the mayor's maid,
you sailed for the new world by yourselves;
longed for your Belfast families; stayed.

You brought two snapshots of the Causeway;
combs — one silver, two tortoiseshell;
a hard conviction that the pint,
or one cigarette, could lead to Hell.

You taught my mother not to whine,
never to lie. She was to brush her hair
one hundred strokes; act "ladylike";
sit up straight in every chair.

(Only in my mother's dreams
could she shake at you a matted mane,
swing like a gibbon through the woods,
wreck her best shoes in pouring rain.)

I can tell you that the little girl
you cared for never has disobeyed;
she still feels you watching her,
shades under the umbrella's shade;

if she got an urge to throw a plate,
sit down for days, do nothing but cry,
she'd see your bone needles flashing
out of the corner of one eye,

tell over gifts from Providence,
tuck each graying, wispy hair
back into place; start a new task;
make those stooping shoulders square.

THREE WOMEN, NURSING HOME, MEDICAL WING

1. *Two Dreams*

I dreamt that they had buried someone else
in *my* plot, the one I'd bought and paid for!
I talked to someone raking at that graveyard —
I couldn't see his eyes behind his shades.
He took my hand and said they'd find me room.

I was hunched in the first seat of an express
rattling past a harbor at two a.m.
Freezing wind kept blasting through the car.
I took a lace-edge hankie from my purse
and draped it, like a veil, across my face.

2. *Prairie Childhood*

We were three of us on a horse, riding to school,
my brothers wearing floursack shirts.
The route took thirty minutes or so,
but if we set out on foot we often got stuck
halfway there in drifts of new snow.

A week after she gave birth,
I remember Ma, on the back porch,
picking off prairie chickens with a rifle.
I had my tonsils out on the sewing table;
she sat up with me the entire night.

The hoboes who asked to pick the wheat
that harvest-time wore thin cotton gloves.
How their hands bled! Pa bandaged them,
found shoes for the boys with blistered feet.

3. *The Gardener's Daughter*

I am not ready to go, not yet.
I have amends to make with my mother.
I need to confess a lie I told.

I'd like to smell lilacs by our front door,
wake up in my childhood home
(only a few flagstones are left of the path).
I'd like to pick berries this June with my father.

I am not ready to go, not yet.
But I'm falling asleep in this field of poppies,
and their blue scent is hurrying me away.

TWO MONUMENTS

1. The Tomb of the Unknown Soldier

White marble. Rolled sod.

Black-shod guard: shining shoes
glide up and down red carpet.

The steed's bronze lip disdainfully curls.

Inside a colonnaded rotunda,
under a Latin diadem,
cases of medals and rosettes.

2. Battlefield

One-room museum:
a letter from an eighteen-year-old, bragging
we'll whup 'em yet!

His dingy, bullet-shredded epaulet.

The wire-rim glasses and dogeared Bible
of the grandmother who refused to leave her house
when the battle started.
(She died at noon under an exploding shell.)

A grasshopper, clinging to a swaying stalk.

A mower roaring over the field.

WAYS OF GOING

for Steve

Will it be like paragliding —
gossamer takeoff, seedlike drifting down
into a sunlit, unexpected grove?

Or skijumping — headlong soaring,
ski-tips piercing clouds,
crystal revelations astonishing my goggles?

Maybe I'll exit with the nonchalance
of a ten-year-old skateboarder,
wheels' down-the-hill my bravura farewell.

Or shimmy into the afterworld,
salsa dancer on a flatbed truck —
maracas coda, bangles flashing
as the parade lurches around the corner.

With sudden relief: a tortoise that had scrabbled
over a stony beach, flippers slipping and flailing,
splashes home in a graceful slide.

Skittery flicker of a glare-weary lizard
startled into the sheltering wings of a leaf,

rusting freighter with a brimming hold
shimmering onto a crimson edge. . . .

Sad rower pushed from shore,
I'll disappear like circles summoned
by an oar's dip.

However I burn through to the next atmosphere,
let your dear face be the last thing I see.

1.

Scene from a romance: rambling through the wood,
suddenly I stumble across a giant.
"Are you a creature of good?" You nod.
Together we adventure to the next scene.

2.

The kitten that followed you home one day —
how did it scent your benevolence?
Tentative shadow glimpsed through the screen,
shyly at dusk it would slip from the curb,
ears radaring forward when it caught your tone,
nuzzling your gentling fingertips.

Fifteen years later, each time I appear
you set down bowl after bowl for me.

3.

What would I find, touring your sweet head?
Nooks packed with facts, quartz-glitters of wit,
green terraces orderly thoughts plash down;
knowledges bundled, a forklift memory
to scoop them out. Scenes with cousins; alcoves
cluttered with dumptrucks, bubblegum cards,
pâpier-maché models — Saturn, Mars, Earth —
plastic weaponry, a catcher's thumped glove.
Quiet zones like pools we found up the mountain,
truths as plain as a prairie sky.

4.

I moved west to join you with what I could lug
in one stuffed suitcase. Coyotes yowled
from salmonberry clumps, minor alps loomed
at our street's end. Rain pattering on grape,
twinflower, bedstraw, bird's-foot trefoil —
every moment sponsored new blossoms.
Marsh wren swaying in a barely-tethered nest
on our cattail stalk, I clung, bowed, sang.

5.

Minarets shimmying in mauve pools . . .
Jahan, you have nothing on my edifice,
this perfect dwelling I've designed for Steve.
The former tenant, a book-collector,
left basement troves we're still discovering —
eighteen-clause titles, rococo colophons.
Our chimney bricks are precisely aligned
so winds play themes from Mozart concerti.
Self-cleaning gutters, lawnmowing sheep. . . .
Miraculous for a temperate climate,
our back yard sports a banana tree;
you pluck your snack each night from its fronds.
Birds of paradise nest in our eaves.

6.

Driving cross-country, in the prairie center,
I leapt out to capture a sunset blaze
and snapped you instead, poised at the wheel.
How many crumpled maps have I squinted at
on long peregrinations north, south, east?
Let me accompany you everyplace,
imp of the gas-cap, glove-compartment gnome —
glance in your rear-view, you'll catch me winking,
flip down the sunshield, I'll slip to your wrist;
tune the radio above the stations
past static-crackle, then hear me hum.

7.
Pink "Stargazers," white lilies you planted
that spring brocaded the garage's hem;
dabbing in each with affectionate thumbs,
you coaxed up seedlings an eyelash wide.
And that dahlia that tried so hard to live!
Translucent fist-bud almost pulsing,
it looked like it would burst, aching green.
The light-ration dwindled, but it stretched, leaned, craned
till even the sturdy chestnut-trees flared.
Hoping for petals till the very last,
swivelling, basking under your smile,
if I had to go, I would yearn toward you.

8.
Travel memories: thatch, oriels —
we would have been peasants in the Old World,
you monitoring a herd of deer
in a sullen drizzle; evenings I'd have shone
the master's salt cellars, scraped blobs of wax
from a Great-Hall sconce. But together we'd have crept
along draughty halls under long-nosed portraits
when the lord was riding, to his library:
mysteries of minuscule; parchment grails.
In the Brueghel painting of the villagefest,
everyone's armwrestling, leapfrogging, whacking a ball;
we hunch on stumps teaching ourselves to read.

9.
Exchanging jokes no one can overhear —
me trailing robes, you flourishing a hat —
we embrace in the parchment initial's ring.
Or, crimson birds with implausible tails,
we go on calling across the margins
over Gothic letters of a *demande d'amour:*

"Who was the most free?" Arveragus
or Dorigen? You're first — no, you are, dear . . .
we tumble in a lattice of forget-me-nots.

10.

Our particular parliament of fowls:
each year, southering from Siberia,
squawking the whole three thousand miles,
the snow geese glide to Vancouver marsh.
What are they doing so far from home,
skidding amid these alien pumpkins?
Basking in the shallows, they gab and gab,
weary, weary — yet they mate for life.
— No hemlock owls bearing swooping doom,
but paired bald eagles in pine candelabra:
I want that for us, leisure, long views,
sharing through decades one dauntless raft.
— The yellow-headed blackbird, once-a-life vision:
gold vouchsafed on a rusting sedge.

11.

Whenever you look up, there I shall be —
and whenever I look up, there will be you
said Gabriel Oak to Miss Everdene,
the wild girl who didn't have the wisdom
to curl with her shepherd by the inglenook.
He sought her when she was lost and silly,
not for a pen but to set her free.

— I stumble in, shaky on my legs,
I nestle in the crook of your arms.

12.

And I have found Demetrius like a jewel,
Mine own, and not mine own. Yes, you are both,
rare nugget blazing in the general slab,
coveted, safe in my pouch of a heart;
fortuitous prize whose shine I want to share
with others who admire its brilliance too.
Untarnished, rustproof, through fire and ice
your adamant lasts. Glinting on my finger
I wear a hint of you, etched "Courage, Truth, Love."

13.

Our idea of paradise: a night at Stuart's —
café of wobbling tables, coffeemaker lamps,
choice of paperbacks comfortably slumped,
students gnawing pens on scraped velvet chairs.
The nearby pawnshop is stacked with striped frisbees,
tie-dyes are fluttering by the Seed 'N Feed.
Chocolate cake, two forks; folksinger twanging —
here I can almost pretend we're twenty,
we've just escaped home, we've got enough verve
to light city blocks. All these years with you!
A sense of infinite possibility
flares before me as you touch my hand.

14.

Let's age together like old-growth trees,
our knobby elbows sueded with moss,
draped over each other in a tipsy embrace
like a couple after their thousandth waltz.
Woodpecker pendants, mushroom-studded ankles,
we'll toast each year with another ring,
welcome hawks like finials to our balding heights.

When the end comes, shall we crash to earth
as comic and good-natured about it

as the bridal couple in the video
toppling as they tango the town-hall floor?
Thudding to the ferns, we'll sleep like spoons again,
looped with huckleberry, frogs booming at our feet,
nurse-logs to saplings bowering a new age.

EPITAPH FOR DIANE

for Diane Jarvis Hunter

She thrust herself at life, a honeybee
thorax-deep in each quivering corolla;
flew pollen-spangled each day back to the hive.

She was willing, too, to go with what might happen
like seeds of roadside grass on Fortune's scarf —
borne off to be sown elsewhere, and grow new.

DISLOCATIONS

During the last hurricane
an iguana
found only on one atoll
was pitched with his comfy palm

and swept bobbing over the Caribbean
to another landfall,
where when he debarked
he discovered he was the only one of his kind.

The monarch aiming for Mexico
winds up in Vegas,
this bug that inched into a shipment of tires
at Hialeah
is sniffing the Montreal runway with bewildered antennae;

you're a seed snagged
in a cat's whisker,
a nub of pollen
saddlebagged by a bee
that bumbled into an orchid
thinking — it had the right markings —
it was his beloved. . . .

Tipped on the sidewalk
like a tree with its root-ball
swathed in burlap,
your tendrils
tangle so tightly around themselves
they refuse the offerings
of the new soil.

What a surprise
to discover
that after all
you're bound to leaf:

if the walls won't stay where they
are, you learn, like Astaire, to flourish across the ceiling;

this starling's heritage
may have been to nibble dropped brioches
in the Tuileries, but
look at her now, making a virtue of necessity
with a bag of cheesecurls in the Bronx.

Already you're a hybrid,
you feel your strengths intermingling
like rivers braiding,
you're startled as the young tree
that suddenly keeps finding peaches at the end of its limbs.

THREE

INSIGHTS

for Derry Lubell

They arrive unbidden
on nobody's schedule
acorn-size illuminations
plinking into your lap

often incongruous
as if some many-hued wine
variegated the last slurp of pop in your can

anonymously distributed
as flyers shoved into your chest on the street
cometlike
occasionally they flicker forward in schools

frequently they unscroll themselves
when you are in the middle of something else —
you're gasping as Pavarotti hits a high note from Paris
and a tornado warning flashes across the screen
you're a bear ambling around a campsite
and suddenly you get lucky: a cooler!
or, among the day's usual receipts,
out of the blue you're handed a ticket to agony

the plates of your being tilt
relationships may quiver
like the parts of a mobile trembling
into a new suspension
the fine guy-wires
tethering you to your current life
are loosened   tautened

they ping gently like windchimes
with earlier visitations

sometimes unwelcome in their initial offerings
fended off like malarial mosquitos
only later do they appear
in their true guise —
the butterfly that applauded on your blistered toe
when you were straining up that mountain

parachutes jerking open
the silken rustle of their sudden knowledge
depositing you in a changing field

REJECTION-SLIP RUMBA

Another box crammed with SASEs,
"we cannot use this at this time,"
"thank you for your interest" —
a volley of dings,
my stamps' hopes cancelled with "we're sorry."

I huff off to the harbor —

and halt
by the delicious reek of fish.

If Neruda could write
an Ode to a Large Tuna,
why should I be discouraged?

No use acting like the crabs
scrabbling for that bucket's lip,
maneuvering like boxers, claws all brag,
or those gulls squawking each other off
that moldy pedestal of piling.

I can thrive on attar of mud
and those tingling shingles of sunlight on the water.
A million distractions
wait to shake out their wings like butterflies.
I'll lounge under this blowing cottonwood
and be laurelled with its white excelsior,
wait breathless like that heron
peering for gifts in the next wave.
Gold leaves whirl into my lap like medallions,
this pile of dirt has something to confide.
Let me attend to that ant there —
she might be Scheherezade.

INSPIRATION

It starts with some tiny fanfare,
a pheromone
piping you like an ant
to a sugar cube;

a waiter at a wedding whirls to your elbow
bearing a telling morsel,

invisible delegates
proffer a seedpod
(hairy, chartreuse),
the expedition's prize;

anonymous benefactors
feed nuggets of bullion
into your night-deposit —
capital to draw on later,
stuccoed all over with interest —
faces, rages, a feather.

One day a scent that had been folded softly away
beeps
through later avalanches of ephemera,

the rare varied thrush
"usually seen only at higher elevations"
flashes its orange
throat in your maple
long enough for a few notes to be transcribed;

the cranial weather propitious,
synapses zip messages cell to cell
like confidences exchanged over a Dutch door;

half-lines drift like cirri into your atmosphere,

some gentle usher
invites you to sit down,
your head inclined like a tulip's
over the white page —

now hope the prevailing wind
shakes loose a scatter of gold.

PUBLISH OR PERISH

My *primum mobile* is almost pure whim
vaguely adulterated by the idea of a schedule.
I won't be hurried any more than a tortoise
heaving itself up a beach to lay eggs once a year.
Ask for a book, I'll give you a scroll
with one haiku revised four hundred times.
I might produce emotions in different hues
than any I had ever experienced,
none of which can be caught on your spectrographs.
I might cross-index scores of references,
and then, deciding all must be destroyed,
carry my oeuvre, unsentimental, to the town dump.
This wad of pollen I'm due to make honey
may have been rationed for me from the start.
And who are you to override my Queen's decree?
I will lounge by the moat, track the progress
of indolent clouds . . . till inspiration beckons
casual as a robin lighting on a wire,
and these tiny hammers start pounding again.

UNKNOWN ARTISTS

1.

In the picture snapped at the festival,
she's standing, fifth row, twenty-fourth from left,
her face partly hidden by someone's fedora.

2.

She bourréed, stage left to right, in *The Nutcracker*.

3.

He daubed a cow's haunch into a master's Nativity.

4.

For an August *Figaro*, she lobbed her notes
with the chorus's into a pink-swirled sky.

5.

The viola part she played at her quartet's recital
was carried home that night, by a whistling couple.

6.

His winged saint, like a nuthatch inching down a pillar
(fourteenth century, "from the workshop of")
survived in one corner of a dim museum
open twice weekly at the curator's discretion.

7.

The red scalloped tails of the kissing birds
she'd inked on the baptismal scrips
for that Mennonite child, circa 1810,
were admired again when a grizzled farmer,
rummaging in his great-uncle's cabinet,
unrolled them, presented them to the town hall.

8.
One poem he wrote was glanced at by a student
riffling through a book, looking for something else,
in the clammy stacks of her college library;
like a purple lupine by a hiker's dusty boot,
it pleased her and refreshed her, before she trudged on.

For once the bus hadn't been late.
She pressed "Up" at half-past eight,
boarded, stood with averted eyes
as the panelled cage began to rise.
She watched the gleaming silver doors
parting to show identical floors
painted a flat oyster white,
pebble-gray rugs, fluorescent light . . .
a briefcase and a tote stepped off.
Someone in front stifled his cough.
Every week the agency sent
her somewhere new. At Capital/Hente,
she hunched at a computer screen,
circling wholesale orders in green.
At Sadwell-Smythe she answered phones
in their blush-pink marble lobby, alone.
For Prudence Insurance, nine to three,
she tapped in data on an old PC
(hospital stays, rations of pills).
At the gas company she issued bills.
Every week, at each new place,
she'd smile at an adjacent face,
people who might or might not say "hi"
when, going for coffee, they rushed by.
Lunch was a sandwich wrapped in foil,
a can of cola that quietly boiled;
by two she'd swept her desktop clean.
She knew the quirks of copy machines,
she had paced hundreds and hundreds of miles
fetching, replacing needed files,
taking notes in boardrooms with model ships,
reordering the paperclips
the V.P. liked, retrieving faxes,

proofreading printouts on sales taxes. . . .
This building had a penthouse garden
where you could light up. At 3:10
she stepped out between potted trees
and concrete benches. The wan breeze
blew soot her way. Gray, glossy, dun,
skyscrapers fenced each horizon.
Sparrows pecked at croissant crumbs;
some giant generator thrummed.
3:25, back at her station,
she doublechecked the pagination
of reports that had to be couriered
by 4 p.m.; retyped a word;
glanced at her book for tomorrow:
Twelfth Street, tenth floor, D. F. Snow.

Grocery-checkstand
pair of hands:
staring down,
she scans, she scans,
chocolate bars,
a dozen cans
of "French-style" peas,
jars — mayo, jam . . .
schooled to please
customers shifting
foot to foot —
Good morning, ma'am!
Pound of lard,
celery, cola —
barely twenty-one,
no time to scan
— a pack of gum,
debit card —
a human face,
no moment free
to ask the regular
how she is,
the muttering man —
Your Time is Money!
Our checkers' speed
is guaranteed!
Six ears of corn —
worked here three years,
(her mother was
a checker too)
— frozen poundcake —
no better jobs
except the mill.

Powdered milk,
"Improved! NEW!"
puppy kibbles,
large squeeze
bottle of cheese
with coupons
FREE!
a pack of Trues,
crisp new bills.
Eight customers
watch her arrange
the eggs, the cans,
potato chips
in the plastic sack
and hand them back.
No change today?
No, no change.

EXILE

I wake up thinking I hear my mother
going downstairs to put the water on,
but it's the landlord fumbling with the boiler.
I haul up the treasures of my old life
and count them over, too many times a day.
Each night I dream the maples at home,
witnesses of so many midnight thoughts,
bend over me, murmuring, benevolent.
Tomorrow I will wake to my favorite bird,
breakfast with brothers volleying jokes.
My cousins will arrive; at dusk we'll play
the usual Red Rover — "Come *over!*" — in the yard.
We'll fall asleep to varying snores;
toward morning, if there's a sudden squall,
my uncle will get up and latch every screen.

I wish I could bask in the raucous vowels
I heard in my classmates' voices at school,
lie in long grass on a spring evening
and smell the dirt I learned baseball on.
I want to sit face to face with the friend
who remembers me stuck in her parents' oak
at a birthday party thirty years ago.
I want to cruise roads familiar to me,
in their ups and downs, as a favorite song —
where one brother, yelling, taught me to shift gears.

In a graveyard here the other day I saw
two tombstones; after the pitted names
they said "Born in," and then my city.
They'd been in this country for fifty years,
and their feet weren't even facing toward home.
Plovers return to beaches where they hatched,

limpets to crevices on bedrock boulders —
I wish I could pick up the continent's edge
and pull this city closer to my first,
marry Hesperus to an eastern star,
jet both my worlds to the wedding feast —
Chesapeake crabs, Kelowna chardonnay,
a cardinal cheering in Western cedar. . . .
Last night I dreamed I phoned my cousin;
"Hello!" she said. "Remind me who you are?"

On "Repose of Rivers" by Hart Crane

"What's the plot?
The Mississippi flowing to the sea,
and Crane going from childhood to death.
One of his clearest and his greatest poems,
much quieter than the other we just read.
The river speaks the poem;
the river's washing out to sea
like your own life — the river's doomed,
all childhood memories, washing out to sea
to find repose. The sapphire's the sea,
remorseless, sinister, hard. Angels might
flake sapphire — that might be one of their jobs.
He's taunting you with paradise.
The willows do hold steady sound, and yet
they don't; the sea's fulfillment of a kind,
the end of life. . . . Don't read this just as death-wish;
Crane was unusually full of life."

On "The Yachts" by William Carlos Williams

"This starts as terza rima; here his lines
are much longer than usual. Very few poems
attempt a narrative; you have to do it
plainly, like a sports reporter would.
Is it a satire, against yachts? Or are
they made quite beautiful? What's horrible
about the race, the competition?
(I think he must have watched basketball games.)
The yachts here could be women, thoroughbreds —
anything beautiful trampling over all
it doesn't notice. Beauty's terrible,

expensive, skillful. . . .Very beautiful
careful description . . . 'arms' . . . they're desperate. . . .
Greeks when they sank a ship mowed the survivors
down, or speared them; the yachts just pass over.
Seems supernatural, doesn't it?
                                      These two
extremes of writing, Williams, Crane — do you
imagine Crane was maddened by this stuff?
He rather liked it, though. Crane could never
describe a yacht, and Williams thought
he was all rhetoric.
                                 Two modernists:
Williams was breaking old metrical forms,
and using new material; Crane had read
Rimbaud, brought thunder and obscurity."

On "Out of the Cradle Endlessly Rocking" by Walt Whitman

"Most operatic thing he ever wrote,
a tour de force, probably about something. . . .
What? — I mean personal. Two thrushes, one dies:
imagine someone Whitman was in love with,
lost. The beginning's all one sentence, highly
organized musically, but loose writing,
as Whitman practiced. Tempting to scan; you can't.
The cradle is the sea . . . it's very odd,
original without one's knowing why.
If you want to say these things, it's falling rhythm.
The ostensible sorrow is the boy
Discovering death, desertion. . . . (I'd
be talking through my hat, if I had one on.)
And often rhythmical musical things
aren't good, they're padding for not feeling. What
prevents that here? It's awfully eloquent
wherever you pick it up. 'From such as now
they start the scene revisiting': this has

74

a tender Pindaric grandeur — I don't know
if you can say that. It's about a child —
that's not a Whitman subject, childhood.
　　His saddest poem in some ways. Hard to think
that birds meant very much to him. . . ."

On "Goodbye My Fancy" by Walt Whitman

"'Goodbye My Fancy' he intended as
his last poem . . . you're too sick to write your last
poem, when the time comes. Clear and elegant —
except for some of the language, and the meter,
it could be seventeenth-century.
Your eyes water, reading it."

PHILOSOPHICAL ARGUMENTS

You are ushered expeditiously through the average
down immaculate halls of a Roman austerity
until you are guided into the presence of the
Conclusion, enthroned.

Solid samples can be Bauhaus-predictable —
you watch the next *whereas*
being hauled into place like
a hunk of prefabricated pyramid.

Sophisticals may awe the uninitiate
like Piranesi *carceri:*
pillared pomp and rhetorical balustrades
flourishing upward to no landing.

The spurious quiver, particleboard amalgams,
reproduction façades lit by ersatz lampposts
a challenger could dismantle with a
snort.

But then there are those
with thousands of years of graffiti
curlicuing their porticoes —

discipular additions
dot their domains like huts,

paragraphs are
balconies; pages,
plazas;

at the fountain court in the center, pilgrims —
the student shoehorned into the required course,
the mother at night-school, the seeker, the browser,
the plumber logging on from the Yukon —

cup their hands and taste
and see their dwelling-place for the first time.

DISPLAY CASE, COUNTY MUSEUM, WASHINGTON STATE

Objects labelled "Souvenirs of the World":

Three mastodon teeth;
a rock from "the ruins of Nineveh";
pebbles from "Solomon's quarry";
chunks of "Jacob's well";
teak ripped from the rail of a British prison ship;
vertebra and anklebone, supposedly Philip the Second of France's;
pocked posts trucked from the old stockade;
a threadbare cougar, stuffed, shot on Mount Olympus;
from the 1860s' White House, rusting bolts;
slate pencils fused in the Chicago Fire;
and, from the founder's great-uncle's migration-ride West,
sickles; a Bible; bullets; nails.

TWO SCENES FROM PHILADELPHIA

1. *Valley Forge, 1777-1778*

Thanksgiving rations, the second year of the war:
a quarter-cup of rice, a dash of vinegar.

Twenty-five barrels of flour, twelve thousand men.
One feasted for two days on a fist-sized pumpkin.

Sentries stood on their hats to warm their feet;
the officers' horses shuddered under needling sleet.

One of three soldiers wintering lost his life.
New Year's morning, a ten-year-old played the fife.

2. *Victorian Interior*

The French windows were swathed with mauve-gray drapes,
ends gathering on plum rugs in velvet folds
reflected in a twelve-foot gilt-framed mirror
above the stag's head on the étagère,
black, lacquered cabinets japanned with ivory,
a pinch-stitched mauve petitpoint fireplace screen.
Carved rosettes above brass chandeliers
which Belfast maids kept glinting with their dusters
trapped, in their arabesques, each gram of soot.
Silver brushes etched with swirled initials
lay poised by "hair receivers" on vanities —
crystal jars for collecting straying wisps
to be woven into wreaths or framed in jet.
The door to the master-bedroom's marbled bath
was diamonded with ruby stained-glass panes;
on the rosewood desk's ebonized veneer,
Trollope was propped with guides to English dogs.

RUIN

Boulevards with planted medians,
hotels like perfume boxes
strewn around the landscape,
a pink mall looming by a lagoon —

the tourists set out for jungle
on a new road
laid like electrical tape
through the trees.

Cola trucks veered past,
their bottles jumping.
Chickens turning circles
in muddy yards,

cul-de-sac,
lake,
white pigs snuffling
in the dirt —

the group bought tickets
at a shed
shading packets of film
on a styrofoam cooler.

Birdsong tinging,
bright beads of water —
they plunged under
branches swagged

with Spanish moss —
ancient rains
that had caught and frayed —
posed by a stela,

fumbled deeper —
"There!" "I saw it first!"
Two hundred feet high,
white stone sown with green.

They clambered up.
From the pyramid's top
all they could see
was slash-horizon,

green pelt bunching
on the land's back.
The guidebook said
towns thousands of years old

lay clenched underneath.
— Down again, at the cola stand:
a sad-eyed monkey
scampered the length

of his twine leash,
dropped to his haunches.
Long, elegant fingers,
a baby's nails —

someone offered a sip
from her bottle of water.
He tilted it, took a swig.
Her piece of egg he threw in the dirt.

On their way back
they snapped a jaguar
crouching to keep its balance
in the bed of a pickup.

1. *School Library*

Sprawled under the Danish-modern tables,
we'd bivouac, provisioned with a shelf's load.
We'd bask below a cat's grin beaming like a planet,
inhale the waft from chocolate waterfalls,
eddy along an unfamiliar river
recumbent on a single leaf.

2. *Midnight Library*

Every night I would tiptoe off
into thickets beckoning around my bed.
Mice in berets hailed me from the wainscot,
a spider floated past waving three legs,
tigers' eyes gleamed, molten discs.
In the morning all was replaced and parklike,
my snail's smudged signature hardly visible,
my moth's-wing powder gilding a few leaves.

3. *Town Library*

Away from the blinding stripe of beach
with its riffle of surf,
the whack*ding*, whackwhackwhack*clang*!
of the pinball arcade,
the tinny insidious transistors with their Top Fortys,
I sat in the basement of the town hall
overhearing only a riffle of pages.
No fizz of cola tickled my nostrils,
just the edgy ichor of rubber cement
as I bandaged splaying spines, pasted due-date slips.
Sightseeing boats
bobbed around the cape,
beachcombers wielded metal-detectors like dowsers,

trawlers chugged in, holds flipping with silver —
quartermaster of my stash of bullion,
I nudged new islands every day,
with Queequeg I saw Leviathan breach,
voices in the leaves I turned over while shelving
kept iridescing into each other
like peacock opals in abalone shells.

4. *College Library*

I never lingered in the reading-room
on cracked leather chairs, under varnished portraits,
but rapelled directly into the stacks' ravines.
Batlike I tuned my ears to the quires,
alighted here and there in ambrosial must.
I parted folios that had not been flicked
by reading fingers in a hundred years,
made my way up at midnight clutching
a week's worth of trophies, fistfuls of sheaves.

5. *Vancouver Library*

Now in a temperate, rain-hushed city
under a stuttering, bluish glare,
I lie down beside teeming shelves
as I first did thirty years ago,
ready to record once more, in my soul's soft tablet,
truths calling among the leaves.

Notes

Dedication

"He was a verray parfit, gentil knyght" — Chaucer, General Prologue, *The Canterbury Tales.*

On the Road to Emmaus

"Landscape with Christ and Two Disciples on the Road to Emmaus" (c. 1535), which hangs in the Los Angeles County Museum of Art, is by Herri met de Bles (c. 1485–c. 1550), a landscape painter who often portrayed Biblical scenes in contemporary Flemish settings.

The Book of Steve

1. "Are you a creature of good or not?" — adapted from Chrétien de Troyes, *Yvain.* In this romance, someone wandering through a forest meets a giant and asks him this question.
5. Shah Jahan — the builder of the Taj Mahal.
9. *Demande d'amour* — This term is used for questions sometimes posed in medieval courtly literature, intended to provoke a discussion from the audience listening to the narrative being read aloud.
"Who was the most free?" — Chaucer, "The Franklin's Tale." In Chaucer's usage here, "free" meant "generous." This *demande d'amour* was also a common folklore motif ("Which was the Noblest Act?").
11. "Whenever you look up, there I shall be. . . ." — Hardy, *Far From the Madding Crowd.* This is what Farmer Gabriel Oak says to Bathsheba Everdene when he first proposes to her.
12. "And I have found Demetrius like a jewel. . . ." — Shakespeare, *A Midsummer Night's Dream*, IV.i.191-2.

Rejection-Slip Rumba

Pablo Neruda (1904 – 1973) –- Chilean poet who wrote odes on many subjects.

Exile

Kelowna — wine-producing region of British Columbia.

Four Lectures by Robert Lowell, 1977

As a student in classes taught by Robert Lowell (1917-1977), I took detailed notes on his remarks about nineteenth and twentieth-century writers. When in a poetry seminar a few years later I was asked to write a dramatic monologue, I put some of Lowell's words into verse.

Philosophical Arguments

Giovanni Battista Piranesi (1720–1778) — Italian designer, etcher, engraver, and architect, who published in 1749–1750 a series of prints, "Invenzioni capric di carceri," depicting fantastical prisons.

Carmine Starnino, Editor
Michael Harris, Founding Editor

SELECTED POEMS David Solway
THE MULBERRY MEN David Solway
A SLOW LIGHT Ross Leckie
NIGHT LETTERS Bill Furey
COMPLICITY Susan Glickman
A NUN'S DIARY Ann Diamond
CAVALIER IN A ROUNDHEAD SCHOOL Errol MacDonald
VEILED COUNTRIES/LIVES Marie-Claire Blais (Translated by Michael Harris)
BLIND PAINTING Robert Melançon (Translated by Philip Stratford)
SMALL HORSES & INTIMATE BEASTS Michel Garneau
   (Translated by Robert McGee)
IN TRANSIT Michael Harris
THE FABULOUS DISGUISE OF OURSELVES Jan Conn
ASHBOURN John Reibetanz
THE POWER TO MOVE Susan Glickman
MAGELLAN'S CLOUDS Robert Allen
MODERN MARRIAGE David Solway
K. IN LOVE Don Coles
THE INVISIBLE MOON Carla Hartsfield
ALONG THE ROAD FROM EDEN George Ellenbogen
DUNINO Stephen Scobie
KINETIC MUSTACHE Arthur Clark
RUE SAINTE FAMILLE Charlotte Hussey
HENRY MOORE'S SHEEP Susan Glickman
SOUTH OF THE TUDO BEM CAFÉ Jan Conn
THE INVENTION OF HONEY Ricardo Sternberg
EVENINGS AT LOOSE ENDS Gérald Godin (Translated by Judith Cowan)
THE PROVING GROUNDS Rhea Tregebov
LITTLE BIRD Don Coles
HOMETOWN Laura Lush
FORTRESS OF CHAIRS Elisabeth Harvor
NEW & SELECTED POEMS Michael Harris
BEDROCK David Solway
TERRORIST LETTERS Ann Diamond

THE SIGNAL ANTHOLOGY Edited by Michael Harris
MURMUR OF THE STARS: SELECTED SHORTER POEMS Peter Dale Scott
WHAT DANTE DID WITH LOSS Jan Conn
MORNING WATCH John Reibetanz
JOY IS NOT MY PROFESSION Muhammad al-Maghut
    (Translated by John Asfour and Alison Burch)
WRESTLING WITH ANGELS: SELECTED POEMS Doug Beardsley
HIDE & SEEK Susan Glickman
MAPPING THE CHAOS Rhea Tregebov
FIRE NEVER SLEEPS Carla Hartsfield
THE RHINO GATE POEMS George Ellenbogen
SHADOW CABINET Richard Sanger
MAP OF DREAMS Ricardo Sternberg
THE NEW WORLD Carmine Starnino
THE LONG COLD GREEN EVENINGS OF SPRING Elisabeth Harvor
FAULT LINE Laura Lush
WHITE STONE: THE ALICE POEMS Stephanie Bolster
KEEP IT ALL Yves Boisvert (Translated by Judith Cowan)
THE GREEN ALEMBIC Louise Fabiani
THE ISLAND IN WINTER Terence Young
A TINKERS' PICNIC Peter Richardson
SARACEN ISLAND: THE POEMS OF ANDREAS KARAVIS David Solway
BEAUTIES ON MAD RIVER: SELECTED AND NEW POEMS Jan Conn
WIND AND ROOT Brent MacLaine
HISTORIES Andrew Steinmetz
ARABY Eric Ormsby
WORDS THAT WALK IN THE NIGHT Pierre Morency
    (Translated by Lissa Cowan and René Brisebois)
A PICNIC ON ICE: SELECTED POEMS Matthew Sweeney
HELIX: NEW AND SELECTED POEMS John Steffler
HERESIES: THE COMPLETE POEMS OF ANNE WILKINSON, 1924-1961
    Edited by Dean Irvine
FIELDER'S CHOICE Elise Partridge
CALLING HOME Richard Sanger

 Véhicule Press

www.vehiculepress.com